DREAM MERCHANTS

MAKING AND SELLING FILMS IN HOLLYWOOD'S GOLDEN AGE

By Jan-Christopher Horak

International Museum of Photography at George Eastman House

TABLE OF CONTENTS

1. Acknowledgements   3

2. The Dream Merchants: Making and Selling Films in   5
   Hollywood's Golden Age

3. The Dream Merchants: A Visual Narrative   35

4. Exhibition Checklist   75

5. Selected Bibliographies   78

ACKNOWLEDGEMENTS

For over thirty years, the master still books from Warner Brothers' Distribution Office in New York sat, archived but inaccessible, in the vaults of the International Museum of Photography at George Eastman House. The present exhibition and catalogue grew out of the desire to present these important historical documents to a wider audience and announce the fact that with the opening of a new Film Study Center at IMP/GEH, the Warner Brothers Film Stills Collection will be available to film historians and researchers.

"The Dream Merchants: Making and Selling Films in Hollywood's Golden Age" was funded through the generous support of Warner Communications, Inc. and the Eastman Kodak Company. Specifically, we would like to thank Mr. Dean Johnson and Mrs. Mary McCarthy at Warners for their enthusiasm, and Mr. Jorg Agin and Mr. John Spence at Kodak.

A number of individuals and institutions gave their time and support in the initial planning of this exhibition. Leith Adams and Ned Comstock of the University of Southern California, Archives of Performing Arts, Warner Brothers Collections, provided much assistance in procurring documents and photographs, as well as colleagueal advice. Other archives contributing staff and energy included the Princeton University Library, the Academy of Motion Picture Arts and Sciences, and UCLA Library of Performing Arts. Thanks also to Leith Adams and Marc Wanamaker/Bison Archives for the loan of materials.

At Eastman House, I would like to thank Robert A. Mayer, Marion Simon, Rick Hock, Pat Musolf, Grant Romer, Barbara Galasso, Rachel Stuhlman, Kaye MacRae, Lewis Schlitt, and Carolyn Zaft. Special thanks to my wife, Martha Schirn, whose discerning eye assisted in the final selection of images, and rejection of typos.

And finally, this exhibition would not have been possible without the extreme hard work, beyond the call of duty, given by my Curatorial Assistant, Robin Blair Bolger.

INTRODUCTION

Deep layers of magical thinking still remain in the unconscious of modern man, and sometimes on the conscious level, too. But most of us no longer view magic as an operational tool... In Hollywood, however, there appears to be a greater use of magical thinking on a conscious level and as a tool for achieving success than elsewhere in the modern world.[1]

One of the central ironies of the American film industry is that film production is both highly organized and ritualistic. While dependent on the exact coordination of literally thousands of people and the amassing of vast financial resources, the economic success or failure of a film is believed to be a matter of secret formulas, of luck smiling, of timing, talent, and guts.

In its classical phase from the 1920s to the 1950s, Hollywood was a monolithic economic system, a multi-national monopoly of corporations, whose structure of film production, distribution and exhibition was based on laws of scientific management, an intense division of labor, the pioneering use of modern advertising techniques, and complete control of the market. Everything possible was done to minimize risk and maximize profits. Yet, success was always thought of in magical terms. The moguls of the motion picture business never tired of propagating their own Horatio Alger myths of rising from the immigrant slums of the lower East side to the plush offices of Sunset Boulevard. In their press releases they never seemed to be at a loss to explain why a given film could make a fortune, while other, equally well-produced films lost millions, but in fact they seldom knew, except to say they had the right "touch." Naturally, as the captains of America's largest leisure industry, film producers were neither interested in exposing their own ruthless business practices, nor were they willing to undermine the social and economic status quo, despite their working class backgrounds.[2] In this context, their magical mumbo-jumbo about the workings of the film industry can be seen as a strategy common to American management:

The mystification of the production process, the separation of people (both as producers and consumers) from an understanding of this process, may be seen emerging early in the twentieth century... In the productive process itself, one of the characteristics

1. Hortense Powdermaker: *HOLLYWOOD the Dream Factory* (Boston: Little, Brown and Co., 1950), pp. 283-284.
2. According to some historians, the film industry was the fourth or fifth largest in the USA in the 1930s and 1940s, but as Douglas Gomery has shown, this was really only a Hollywood fabrication. In 1937 the film industry placed 45th in gross sales, far behind the auto and steel industries. Douglas Gomery: *The Hollywood Studio System* (New York: St. Martin's Press., 1986).

*of "scientific management" beyond and perhaps more important
than its efficiency, is its separation of the work process from an
understanding of what is being made.*[3]

Hollywood's discourse always supported a romantic mythology, because the very commodity this industry produced was fantasy and fictional narratives. Film images sought to transport an audience from the real world into a universe of myth, where audience desires could find at least partial satisfaction. Long before economists thought in such terms, the film industry offered American consumers a service, leisure time activity, rather than an industrial commodity, and thus foreshadowed the post-industrial, service economy of the late 20th century.

Another irony of Hollywood film production is that while the publicity agents of the dream merchants did their best to present the process of film production as something magical, as a matter of secret codes and immense quantities of money and energy, of great movie stars working in harmony with brilliant directors, those same publicity agents documented in minute detail every phase of production and sales, called "exploitation." The major studios had a photographer on the set of every film. He was responsible for taking stills of the action in front of and behind the camera, in the dressing rooms of the stars, and on the studio lots. Once a film reached the theatres, photographers were on hand to document premieres, publicity stunts, public appearances of the stars, parades, media events in short, the total sum of a film's exploitation. All these images served as possible illustrations for news stories, magazine articles, gossip columns, posters, press books, and other forms of advertising.

The master stills books might contain as many as two or three thousand individual images. Thus, while the master still books of the film companies originally generated newspaper and magazine publicity for a film, and ultimately increased box office sales, they now constitute visual records of Hollywood film production, distribution and exhibition. Reading these publicity images "against the grain" as historical documents, these photographs allow us not only to reconstruct the dream machine and the myths it attempted to produce, but also to get a glimpse of the actual structure of the classical Hollywood studio system.

The Warner Brothers Film Stills Collection at the International Museum of Photography at George Eastman House is a virtually complete record of that studio's film production and exploitation between the years 1925 and 1952. During that time, Warner Brothers grew from a small, independent concern to a major film company, incorporating every level of film production, distribution and exhibition. By 1930 Warner Brothers had joined the ranks of the "five sisters" (Paramount, Metro-Goldwyn-Mayer, Fox Film Corporation, and RKO), all of whom owned not only film production facilities, but also distribution outlets and thousands of movie theatres. The "Little Three" (Universal, Co-

3. Stuart Ewen: *Captains of Consciousness. Advertising and the Social Roots of the Consumer Culture* (New York: McGraw-Hill Book Co., 1977), p. 105.

lumbia, and United Artists), on the other hand, controlled production and distribution companies, while releasing their films to the movie houses of the majors. Through tacit agreement, these companies divided the American and world film markets among themselves, ruthlessly crushing any competitors who posed a threat to their hegemony.

The demise of the studio system came about because of both technological and judicial factors. The Paramount Consent Decree of 1948 forced all the studios to divest themselves of their giant theatre holdings. They could no longer count on cinema owners to buy all their product, whether good, bad or mediocre. Secondly, the growth of the television industry, initially separate from the film industry, contributed to a weakening of the studios, as audiences increasingly turned from film viewing to television as their primary mode of visual entertainment.

After 1948 Warner Brothers was forced to sell off its movie theatres. In the mid 1950s it sold all its pre-1948 films to United Artists. Yet it, like Paramount, 20th Century-Fox, Columbia, and Universal has survived into the 1980s as a film producer and distributor, and as part of a larger media conglomerate. Warner Communications includes film and television interests, publishing houses, cable networks, record companies, music publishing, videotape distribution, and other entertainment service companies, while continuing to operate the Burbank studios (and the old Culver City/MGM/ Lorimar studios) for its own productions and as a rental facility for other producers.[4]

As historical documents the Warner Brothers Film Stills Collection represents the inner workings of a Hollywood film company during its classical phase. In that period the cinema was truly a mass media, rather than one of several entertainment options. Warner Brothers can thus be considered a paradigm for the Hollywood studio system as a whole, giving valuable insight into the structure of the American film industry during the studio era. Its method of working also portends how modern advertising and public relations affect our world today.

It has only been in recent years that a new generation of film historians, for the most part educated in film studies programs at university, has torn away the mythologies of Hollywood's discourse to uncover the presuppositions and strategies governing the production, distribution, and exhibition of film in the United States. Tediously searching out primary resource material in the often dusty recesses of film archives, rather than relying on established canons of thought, these historians have begun to analyze and explicate American film practice by drawing on film company documents, financial and production records, original film scripts, inter-office memos, film publicity materials, industry trade periodicals, legal files, distribution records, and audience analyses. They have thus begun to deconstruct Hollywood's mythology, in order to formulate a history which relates the symbiotic relationships between film technologies and industrial

---

4. As of this writing in March 1989, a merger is planned between Warner and Time Inc. The new Time Warner, Inc. will be the largest media conglomerate in the world with a total stock market value of $18 billion and an annual revenue of $10 billion. "Time Inc. and Warner to Merge, Creating Largest Media Company," in *New York Times*, Vol. 88, No. 47,800 (March 5, 1989), p. 1.

relations, marketing and advertising, filmmakers' intentions and audience reception. Such a history begins to define not only the way in which our present media system has evolved, but also explains the degree to which ordinary lives in America are permeated by mass media-produced desires.

Likewise, the present project proposes to contribute to an understanding of Hollywood as a center of commodity production, distribution, and exhibition, a factory system governed by the laws of scientific management, rationalized labor, and modern advertising. The primary documents used for such an analysis will be film stills, a resource which has been previously under-utilized by film historians. Through photographic images, every phase of film production, from writing scripts to designing sets and costumes, from the actual shooting in the studio and on location, to the post-production phase, involving the editing and creation of special effects and musical tracks, are visualized. Furthermore, these images illustrate the work of the company's distribution and exhibition departments, its publicity machine, including advertising campaigns, press books, fan magazine links, the organization of personal appearances, gala premieres, publicity stunts, and product tie-ins. Thus, the exhibition and catalogue attempt to visualize the Hollywood factory system, and to recover the most public sphere of film culture, giving readers not only insights into the past, but also allowing them to understand those structures and processes which remold our present-day society into the format of "entertainment tonight."

I t is often forgotten that even in their classical phase the Hollywood film studios were often only one economic unit in larger conglomerates, which included banking interests, insurance, publishing companies, and other diverse corporations. The financial clout of the parent companies guaranteed capital for the on-going business of film production. In fact, only five percent of Warner Brothers' capital was tied up in the Burbank film studios and film production. Only about one percent of its business was invested in distribution, while approximately ninety percent of its capital was in exhibition.[5] The remaining percentage points were invested in radio, television, real estate, music publishing and recording, booking agencies, lithography, and theatre supply. Moreover, the film studios often controlled every aspect of film production, including financial interests in film processing laboratories and other support services. By the late 1920s, Hollywood had learned the lessons of scientific management to control capital expenditures, keep organized labor under control, and maximize profits.

This had not always been so. In the earliest period of experimentation between 1895 and 1908, when a first generation of film producers and exhibitors founded film companies as small businesses, the film industry functioned essentially as a cottage industry. The earliest film producers (the Edison Manufacturing Company and the American Mutoscope and Biograph Company) were, in fact, manufacturers of film projectors, who quickly realized that they would also have to supply films for those projectors.[6] By the early 1900s a number of motion picture production companies had come into existence, including Edison, Biograph, Vitagraph, Lubin, Selig, and Melies Star Films, soon to be joined by Powers, Thannhouser, Kalem, Essanay, IMP, Solax, Rex, and probably hundreds of others. Before 1903 producers sold their films outright by the foot, asking exhibitors to pay anywhere from $50 to $100 per title, which were run until the market was saturated.[7] With programs changing at an ever-increasing rate, this system became economically untenable.

According to conventional wisdom, Harry J. Miles of San Francisco came up with a solution to this dilemma in 1902 by purchasing films from the producer and then leasing them to individual vaudeville houses at half price. The development of "exchanges"

5. Anthony H. Dawson: "Motion Picture Economics," in: *Hollywood Quarterly*, Vol. 3, No. 3 (Spring 1948), p. 225.
6. See Charles John Musser: *Before the Nickelodeon: Edwin S. Porter and the Edison Manufacturing Company*. New York University (Ph.D.), 1986; Robert C. Allen: "Vitascope/Cinematographe: Initial Patterns of American Industrial Film Practice" in: *Journal of the University Film Association*, Vol 31, No. 2 (Spring 1979), pp. 13-18, reprinted in: Gorham Kindem (ed.): *The American Movie Industry* (Carbondale: Southern Illinois University Press, 1982).
7. The American Mutascope and Biograph catalogue of 1902 lists several thousand titles. Reprinted in *Thomas A. Edison Papers: Early Motion Picture Catalogues*, Microfilm, Vol. 2.

meant that the distributor maintained film inventories, supervised the handling of films, and attended to the repair of damaged films. The exhibitor was thus relieved of these costs, without cutting into the profits of the producer.[8] By 1907 more than 130 exchanges operated in various parts of the country.

Initially films were projected only as an adjunct to live vaudeville performances. Many early films featured "canned" performances of well-known vaudevillians. It is still a matter of historical debate when exactly the first store-front "nickelodeon" theatres opened, where films could be seen for just five cents, rather than the twenty to thirty cents charged by vaudeville houses. Some historians have credited Harry Davis of Pittsburgh, PA. with inventing the term "nickelodeon" in 1905, but it is probable that

The Warner Brothers standing in front of their first nickelodeon in 1907.

early store fronts opened in a number of locations in that year, bearing such colorful names as "Dreamland," "Bijou," "The Princess," "Electric," "Bijou Dream."[9] By early 1907 there were more than 2,500 nickelodeons in the U.S.A., with the number "increasing so rapidly that positive figures are unobtainable."[10] Many of the later movie moguls, including the Warner Brothers (who bought their first theatre in Castle, PA. in 1906), Adolph Zukor (Paramount), Carl Laemmle (Universal), Louis B. Mayer (MGM), William Fox (20th Century-Fox), and Marcus Loew (MGM), began their careers as

8. Howard T. Lewis: *The Motion Picture Industry* (New York: D. Van Nostrand Co. Inc., 1933) p. 4.
9. Q. David Bowers: *Nickelodeon Theatres and their Music* (New York: Vestal Press, Ltd., 1986) pp. 9-51.
10. *Variety*, January 26, 1907, p. 12, quoted in Robert C. Allen: "Motion Picture Exhibition in Manhattan, 1906-1912," in: John L. Fell (ed.): *Film Before Griffith* (Berkeley: University of California Press, 1983), p. 165.

nickelodeon operators, eventually purchasing chains of theatres, exchanges, and production facilities.

Thus, within the first ten years after the invention of motion picture projection, the basic structure of the film industry was in place, divided as it were into production, distribution, and exhibition. The first vertically organized film combine, uniting all three levels of the industry, was formed by Paramount in 1919, followed by Loew's-Metro in 1921. The initial impetus for the Paramount merger was the growing strength of First National, a theatre chain controlling over 639 screens, which had signed Charles Chaplin and Mary Pickford to production contracts, thus threatening Paramount's control over virtually all the major stars. However, it was a financial report by H.D.H. Connick to Kuhn, Loeb and Co. supporting a loan to Paramount that convinced company president, Adolph Zukor, of the wisdom of owning his own theatre chain:

> ... the largest returns of the industry result from exhibiting pictures to the public, not from manufacturing them. The Famous Players-Lasky Corporation Sales Department (Paramount, JCH) estimates that the gross annual return of the 15,000 American theatres during 1919 will be $800,000,000 and that the total amount the producers will receive in the form of sales and leases of film and accessories will not be over $90,000,000. It is apparent to anyone who has had theatrical experience that this is not an equitable division.[11]

A few years later the still upstart Warner Brothers began making plans for moving back into film exhibition, having recently acquired the Vitagraph Distribution Company to augment their Sunset Boulevard production facility. As Harry noted in 1924: "It is not through any wish on our part to enter the exhibiting end of the industry, but it is a protective measure to ourselves..."[12]

The first steps towards creating an industry-wide monopoly of the motion picture industry were taken in December 1908 when Edison and Biograph and their respective licensees formed the Motion Picture Patents Company (MPPC). The trust formalized exclusive trade relations between the most important film producers, all the major exchanges, and the leading exhibition chains, with Eastman Kodak as the sole supplier of raw film stock.[13] Within a few years, however, the trust broke down, not only because independent motion picture producers gained ever more strength, but also because Kodak's agent, Jules Bruletor, decided to sell raw film stock to such independents as Carl Laemmle and William Fox, thus ending any exclusivity rights members of the trust may have had. In any case, the MPPC was struck down by U.S. District Court in 1915, because it was considered in violation of the Sherman Anti-Trust Act. Nevertheless, the

11. Quoted in Mae D. Huettig: *Economic Control of the Motion Picture Industry* (Philadelphia: University of Pennsylvania Press, 1944), pp. 34-35.
12. quoted in Charles Higham: *Warner Brothers* (New York: Charles Scribners & Sons, 1975), p. 41.
13. Ralph Cassady, Jr.: "Monopoly in Motion Picture Production and Distribution: 1908-1915," in: *Southern California Law Review*, Vol. 32 (1959), pp. 325-390, reprinted in Kindem, p. 28.

Patents Company was important, because the structure of its agreements foreshadowed subsequent industry developments:

> ...the structure of the MPPC agreements with its various branches suggests less a quest for total control than a desire to regularize and standardize income, demand, and profits in order to ensure the possibility of long-term planning for a rationalized production.[14]

The Motion Picture Patents Company was the first attempt to move the motion picture industry away from a cottage industry of first and second generation pioneers, independent motion picture directors and producers competing in a relatively open, albeit chaotic, marketplace, towards a highly controlled market dominated by a small group of very large corporations. Control over the means of production rested in the hands of management, while labor was fragmented through a high degree of specialization. Whereas early directors like D.W. Griffith and Maurice Tourneur were primarily interested in producing artistic films, the overriding objective of corporate management was strength, rate of growth and size, all of which were measured by profits.[15]

In order to maximize profits, management had to rationalize production processes, standardizing both the mode of production and the product, while creating consumer needs through the techniques of modern advertising. After 1917, the film industry as a whole, and Warner Brothers in particular after 1925, conformed to American industrial norms by practicing a division of labor, scientific management, and consumer advertising.

For approximately thirty years, during the period known as the classical Hollywood studio era, film companies were allowed to earn unprecedented profits. Their flagrant violations of anti-trust laws were called into question by the U.S. Justice Department as early as the 1920s. The courts continued hearing cases for almost thirty years, before the "Consent Decree" of 1948 effectively ended the monopolistic position of the majors.

In 1921 the Federal Trade Commission had filed its first complaint against Paramount & Co.[16] In 1929, after the acquisition of First National and the Stanley Theatre chain, Warner Brothers was sued under the provisions of the Clayton Act, which forbade the acquisition of any competitor with the intent of creating a monopoly.[17] In a criminal case based on the Sherman Anti-Trust Act, the Justice Department in 1935 charged that Harry Warner, Paramount, and Fox had conspired to deny a St. Louis independent any first run films, thus forcing him from the market. When the government lost the case,

14. Jeanne Thomas Allen: "Afterword" (to Cassady article), in: Kindem, p. 72.
15. Paul A. Baran and Paul M. Sweezy: *Monopoly Capital. An Essay on the American Economic and Social Order* (New York: Modern Reader Paperbacks, 1968), p. 39. On the position of early motion picture directors, see Jan-Christopher Horak: "Good Morning, Babylon. Maurice Tourneur's Battle Against the Studio System," in: *Image*, Vol. 31, No. 2 (September 1988), pp. 1-12.
16. Ernest Borneman: "United States versus Hollywood," in: *Sight and Sound*, Vol. 19, No. 10 (February 1951), p. 419.
17. "New Anti-Trust Drive is Launched on Old Front," in: *Business Week*, No. 14 (December 11, 1929), p. 10; Ralph Culver Bennett: "The Merger Movement in the Motion Picture Industry," in: *The Annals of the American Academy of Political and Social Science*, Vol. 147 (January 1930), pp. 92-94.

they continued to prosecute in a civil suit in two further courts.[18] On July 20, 1938 the Justice Department filed suit against the five majors, accusing them of twenty-eight separate offenses in violation of the Sherman Act, including block booking, blind buying, and the acquisition of theatres for purposes of creating a monopoly. The case was settled out of court, when a "Consent Decree" was reached in November 1940, which limited some practices, but kept the status quo intact.[19] Not until the Paramount Consent Decree of 1948 did the motion picture companies begin the process of divorcement, separating production companies from exhibition. Paramount split in 1949, RKO in 1950, 20th Century-Fox in 1951, and Warners in 1953. Hollywood was never again the same.

18. "Lawsuit in St. Louis," in *Time*, Vol. 26, No. 16 (October 14, 1935); "Warner Brothers," in: *Fortune*, Vol. 16, No. 6 (December 1936), p. 212.
19. Huettig, pp. 140-141.

The Warner Brothers Studio at Burbank, CA. (acquired by Warners within two years of its construction in 1926, when they bought First National) was a self-sufficient city within a city. Warner Brothers also owned small production facilities on Sunset Boulevard (the old W.B. lot) and in Flatbush, New York (the old Vitagraph Studios). Not only did the studio facility at Burbank include sound stages, ready-made Western towns, a New York street, a tenement, a Viennese set, all ready to use on the backlot, [20] but also workshops, bungalows for the stars, restaurants, an infirmary, garages for the transportation department, police and fire departments, film, property, and costume storage areas, administration buildings, screening rooms, and laboratories. While generating a huge overhead, such facilities had the advantage that the company could control every phase of production, without having to rely on outside suppliers. Given the guaranteed market at their disposal, studio overhead was a moot point. At any one time the studios usually had anywhere from thirty to fifty films in various stages of pre-production, production and post-production.

In order for the studio to function efficiently, a high degree of specialization was necessary and desirable, at least from the point of view of management. The process by which any industrial production is divided into an assembly line system, where the individual worker is responsible for only one activity in the production process, was first developed by Frederick Winslow Taylor. It came widely into use in American industry after 1890. In the film industry "Taylorism" was acknowledged to have made its mark in the 1910s when Thomas Ince, among others, divided film production activities among a number of different departments, some directly connected to production, others to management. [21] By the late 1920s this initially rather loose system had evolved into a highly complex division of labor.

The Warner Brothers' Burbank studio, for example, included the following departments:

Advertising Department - Responsible for the commercial advertising work of the studio, including the design of billboards, and the production of trailers.

Art Department - In charge of designing all studio sets and "backgrounds against which the action is photographed," as well as producing all miniatures, mattes, and special effects.

Camera Department - Studio cinematography, the motion picture cameras and equip-

20. Nick Roddick: *A New Deal in Entertainment. Warner Brothers in the 1930s* (London: British Film Institute, 1983), p. 22.
21. Janet Staiger: "Dividing Labor for Production Control: Thomas Ince and the Rise of the Studio System," in: *Cinema Journal*, Vol. 18, No. 2 (Spring 1979), pp. 16-25.

ment involved in cinematography, all art and background titles, and insert cards.

Censorship Department - Responsible for reviewing all scripts before production, as well as acting as a liaison to the Motion Picture Code Authority (Hays Office).

Commissary Department - Managed all commissaries, restaurants, and food services on the studio lot.

Comptroller Group - Directed studio's auditing and accounting, insurance, credit union, and payroll.

Construction Department - In charge of the construction of all sets, coordinating carpenters, painters, plumbers, and plaster shop. Supervised grips, responsible for maintaining and servicing dollies, booms, reflectors, and parallels.

Contract Department - Reviewed all contracts with actors and other talent, as well as other legal matters.

Directors Group - All film directors, dance directors, dialogue directors, assistant directors.

Editors Group - Responsible for film editing, film library stock shots.

General and Production Management Group - Included Jack Warner, producers, assistant and associate producers, studio managers, budget clerks, and an industrial relations manager.

Laboratory Group - processed motion picture negative film, matched picture and track negatives, struck prints, shipping and receiving. Equipment was repaired in the precision machine shop. In the Stills Department, all still photographs for studio publicity and documentation were shot and developed.

Make-Up Department - In charge of designing and applying all make-up and cosmetics, styling and dressing hair.

Mechanical Department - Metalworking craftsmen, electricians, tinsmiths, sheet metal workers, blacksmiths, machinists, foundry workers, and so on.

Music Department- Direction of all musical activity in the studio, including composition and orchestra work.

Plant Engineering and Maintenance Group - Responsible for air conditioning and heating, as well as maintenance of the physical plant, supervision of the Fire Department and Infirmary.

Police Department - In charge of studio security.

Projection Department - all motion picture projection, including rear-projection during production.

Property Department - Responsible for inventories, purchasing, rental and repair, animal trainers and supervisors.

Publicity Department - created publicity directly connected to the studio; a fashion editor, portrait photographers, and unit publicists on staff.

Purchasing Department - Coordinated purchase and distribution of all supplies.

Research Department - All research related to authenticating details, sets, costumes, historical facts used in films.

Scenario Department - Reviewed stories purchased for script development, assigned writers, and produced scripts.

Service Department - Janitorial services, gymnasium, barber shops, mail room, receptionists, messengers, typewriter maintenance, telephones, and telegraph.

Sound Department - In charge of all sound recording.

Stenographic Department - Secretarial services.

Talent Group - Actors, casting directors, talent scouts, drama coaches, school teachers.

Transportation Group - Management and maintenance of automobiles, as well as traffic control on studio lot.

Wardrobe Department - designed, sewed and fitted costumes and accessories.

No less than 558 job descriptions were listed in the "Manual of Motion Picture Job Classifications," not including apprentices, assistants, helpers, and stand-bys.[22] The Music Department, for example, classified the following jobs:

Asst. Head Music Dept.	Music Teacher
Music Director	Vocal Coach
Composer	Conductor
Scorer	Musician
Arranger	Contractor (Music)
Lyricist	Head Music Librarian
Song Writer	Asst. Head Music Librarian
Music Advisor	Copy Dept. Head
Music Teacher	Music Casting Director
Photograph Operator	

From the point of view of management, such a minute division of labor had its advantages. 1) The standardization of work processes increased efficiency by cutting costs due to a lack of uniformity. 2) Single elements of work allowed for exact quality control. 3) Individual workers were given limited responsibility, leaving virtually all decisions to management. 4) An individual was expendable and easily replaced, allowing management to keep both salary demands and labor-management disputes at bay. 5) By centralizing employment within a few studios in the Los Angeles metropolitan area, film companies could institute a blacklist against troublesome employees, thus decreasing irregularities in production.[23]

Less than fifty percent of film industry employees were permanently or even semi-permanently under contract. According to statistics for 1929, the film industry encompassed:[24]

Permanently employed staff	17,614	37.2%
Extras registered with Central Casting	17,541	37.0%
Free-lance players on single picture contracts	2,455	5.5%
Persons engaged outside the studios but wholly dependent on the film industry	9,800	20.6%

Unemployment was, in fact, chronic among all but the most well-known stars and directors: out of the forty-two trade unions with film industry contracts, the studios hired members of forty unions without obligation to guarantee more than one day's employment. Unemployment among painters ran at 56%, of property craftsmen at 36.5%, of

22. Industrial Relations File, Box 1031, Warner Brothers Archive, University of Southern California (WB/USC).
23. See Staiger, p. 17.
24. Arnold Kohler: "Some Aspects of Conditions of Employment in the Film Industry," in: *International Labour Review*, Vol 23, No. 6 (June 1931), p. 780.

sound technicians at 35%. Of 15,000 screen extras who in 1939 worked at least once, 4,564 worked less than ten days. Finally, while two-hundred writers held studio contracts in 1947, approximately 1,300 screenwriters competed for the other two-hundred writing assignments.[25]

Although not directly responsible for Hollywood's division of labor, unions contributed to a further fragmentation of the work process, due to jurisdictional disputes. Unionization came in 1926, when the "Basic Studio Agreement" was signed by nine major producing companies and five unions,[26] as a result of the International Alliance of Theatrical Stage Employees and Moving Picture Machine Operators (IATSE) which had previously unionized projectionists, and could thus threaten to shut down every cinema in the country. While the Basic Studio Agreement divided work among several crafts, new technologies invariably led to competing unions laying claim to new occupations. For example, a 1933 strike centered on a struggle between electrical workers and the IATSE over the unionization of soundmen. Evidence suggests that studio management encouraged jurisdictional disputes, allowing film producers to overload the labor market with replacement workers, thus weakening the bargaining position of any single union.[27]

The principles of scientific management go hand-in-hand with the division of labor. In scientific management, all production decisions are made by management. Industrial knowledge is thus transferred away from the skilled craftsperson towards a "hegemonic reliability of managerial planning and rationalized technology."[28] Scientific management allows corporate managers to develop strategies that maximize company profits by controlling costs for materials and production.

While studio labor was compartmentalized, as a matter of efficiency, the films were standardized, as a matter of cost effectiveness. Film producers realized it was economically advantageous to reutilize costumes and sets, in order to recoup initial investments for construction materials and labor. In the studio era, film companies standardized both the physical plant and the product itself. Certain film genres developed not only because certain kinds of films were popular, but also because of the necessity to produce films as cheaply as possible. In westerns, gangster films, swashbucklers, melodramas, comedies, musicals, and bio-pics, the studio just switched stories, sets, or actors to make a new film. Warner Brothers, in particular, was extremely adept at genre production:

> *Warner pictures are not so much alike as so many Fords but they*
> *are almost as easy to recognize; they lead the low-priced field, and*
> *the profit to Warner is in the volume rather than in an occasional*

25. Quoted in Anthony A.P. Dawson: Hollywood's Labor Troubles," in: *Industrial and Labor Relations Review*, Vol. 1, No. 4 (July 1948), pp. 640-641.
26. The signing unions included IATSE, the United Brotherhood of Carpenters and Joiners, the International Brotherhood of Electrical Workers, the International Brotherhood of Painters and Paperhangers, and the American Federation of Musicians. See Murray Ross: "Labor Relations in Hollywood," in: *The Annals of the American Academy of Political and Social Science*, Vol. 164 (1947), p. 58.
27. Dawson (1948), p. 644. See also Anthony Dawson: "Patterns of Production and Employment in Hollywood," in: *Hollywood Quarterly*, Vol. 4, No. 4 (Summer 1950), pp. 338-353.
28. Ewe, p. 195.

*smash hit... By never buying unnecessary stories, rarely making
retakes, and always knocking temperament on the head where they
can the Warners, get more production money onto the screen than
any other studio.*[29]

If a film story didn't fit a genre category, it probably wasn't made. Stars under contract were assigned similar roles in countless films, character actors stereotyped, writers asked to rewrite successful films. They changed only enough plot to make the film resaleable, while directors specializing in specific genres added visual flair. The studio Publicity Department invented fantastic stories about the lives of the stars, but the reality at Warners was that everyone, including the highest-paid actors, were subject to rigid studio discipline. If they misbehaved by appearing late for work, holding up a production schedule, or by refusing to take on an assigned role, they were fined by studio management, which went to extraordinary lengths to collect even minute amounts of misspent studio cash. Directors or actors who management labelled "difficult to work with," were ruthlessly jettisoned, once their contracts expired. Bette Davis was perhaps the one exception that proved the rule.

Within the studio system, film producers made decisions, rather than directors. Before 1925 directors were the guiding force, choosing not only scripts, but also casting actors, sets and locations, and editing the final cut. Once the studio system was in place, the director was demoted to a position where he/she was merely responsible for the *mise en scene*, i.e., for the direction of actors and the placement of the camera. The many months of preparation, before actors actually came on the set, as well as all the post-production work, after the negative was "in the can," were the responsibility of the producer.

While the salaries of "stars" made the headlines (in fact only a very few stars received astronomical salaries, and usually not for very long), studio bosses and producers were among the highest-paid managers in the nation, receiving executive compensation far in excess of standards set elsewhere in corporate America.[30] For example, Hal Wallis received $208,000 per year in 1942, plus ten percent of all profits on the films under his supervision, or a flat bonus of $25,000 per film.[31] Producing at least four films a year, Wallis probably earned in excess of $300,000 per year, not including such perks as travel, a studio-built projection room in his private residence, and hired help. Likewise, in 1939 the top twenty corporate officers at Warners received 58.3% of the company's net earnings, while common stock shareholders received no dividends.[32]

In contrast, a script clerk earned $50 per week, a stills photographer $85, an assistant director $500, which means that even if these professionals were fully employed (which they seldom were), they earned between $2600 and $26,000 per year. While non-star

29. *Fortune*, (1936), p. 111.
30. Huettig, p. 112; Gomery (1986), p. 7.
31. Hal B. Wallis, Legal File, Box #2819, WB/USC.
32. Huettig, p. 106.

actors received anywhere from $200-3,000 per film, most only made five to six films a year, for a maximum total of $18,000 a year.[33]

Film production schedules and budgets for the year were usually set up in the New York office and then passed on to the studio boss. In Burbank, Jack Warner and his assistants, Darryl Zanuck (1931-33), Hal B. Wallis (1933-44), and Steve Trilling (1944-51), assigned films to individual line producers who were responsible for hiring cast and crews, setting up the daily shooting schedules, getting the films made and ready for release.

A complicated production set-up for SIX DAY BIKE RIDER (1934).

A typical shooting schedule listed every actor on a vertical axis and shooting days/locations on a horizontal axis, allowing the producer to schedule only those actors necessary for a particular day's shoot. For each day of shooting the line producer filled out a "Daily Production and Progress Report," listing exactly when a day's work started and when it was finished, which shots were completed, how many stills were taken, and which staff was on hand, and for exactly how long. The report accounted for every single minute of company time. For example, on the first day of production of *MISSION TO MOSCOW (11-9-1942)*, director Michael Curtiz arrived on location at 7:25 AM, set up the first shot between 7:25 and 8:10 AM, rehearsed with his actors between 8:10 and 8:15 AM, and had the first shot (32 feet) completed at 8:20 AM.[34] Thus, producers kept

33. A MIDSUMMER NIGHT'S DREAM, production file (budget), Box # M105, WB/USC.
34. MISSION TO MOSCOW, production file, Box # 1486, WB/USC.

tabs on their staff, and were ruthless when they felt time had been wasted.

As head of production, Hal Wallis held perhaps the tightest reins, writing an avalanche of memos to his subordinates, while simultaneously keeping track of every production on the lot:

> *... reading original story material, supervising casting and contractual negotiations, attending writer's conferences and commenting on scripts, approving budgets and schedules, viewing the days' rushes and making extremely detailed cutting notes (six pages was not unusual) on the post-production phase.*[35]

The actual purchase of screen stories, whether original scripts, novels, plays, short stories, or magazine pieces, which had proven "track records," was handled by Warner Brothers' Story Department. Headed for many years by Jake Wilk in New York, the Story Department was constantly on the lookout for "hot properties." Bidding between motion picture companies for the screen rights to a particularly successful novel or play was usually intense. Rights sold for as low as $1 to well over $50,000, depending on the agility of the writer's agent.[36] Nevertheless, story costs usually amounted to only a fraction of the production budget, broken down as follows:[37]

Story Costs	5%
Production and Direction	5%
Sets and Properties	35%
Stars and Cast	20%
Studio Overhead	20%
Income Taxes	5%
Net Profits	10%

The process of film production was a highly complex, highly industrialized method of manufacturing, involving thousands of employees and requiring a sophisticated system of management. Yet, studio production accounted for only a minor portion of Warner Brothers total assets and capital. Financial assets and the real power were located in New York, not California. The distribution and exhibition offices of all the motion picture companies were to be found on the East Coast. In the Warners Building on West 44th Street over one thousand employees worked in sales, accounting, legal, real estate, theatre, advertising, publicity, and distribution. It was there that Harry Warner ruled the empire.

35. Roddick, p. 24. See also Jan-Chistopher Horak: "G.W. Pabst in Hollywood or Every Modem Hero Deserves a Mother," in: *Film History*, Vol. 1, No. 1 (June 1987), pp. 54-57.
36. For example, Warner Bros. paid only $1 for Louis Broomfield's popular novel, *A Modern Hero* in 1933, even though Fox had originally paid $20,000, because the latter company was interested in acquiring the rights to a Warners' silent, which it received in the deal. See Horak (1987), pp. 53-64.
37. John George Glover, William Bouck Cornell (ed.): *The Development of American Industries. Their Economic Significance* (New York: Prentice-Hall, 1951), p. 943.

20

E ven though motion picture distribution amounted to just one percent of Warner Brothers' investment, its importance in the chain from producer to consumer was immeasurable. The distributor was not only a middleman, responsible for getting films to theatres, i.e., physically handling the product, but also for selling the product to the public. More than in any other industry, the techniques of modern advertising played a role in selling. The "image" a studio and its stars created through a vast publicity network directly affected its success in the marketplace.

Warner Brothers operated thirty-seven film exchanges in the U.S.A. and Canada. Each was responsible for servicing a certain territory, and employed thirty to forty persons. The exchange got films to a theatre on time, repaired damaged films before they went to the next theatre, and kept up inventories. Warners Distribution rented to approximately 14,000 theatres, not including its own chain of 560 cinemas.[38] Foreign Distribution added another ninety-three exchanges in forty-two different countries.[39] However, almost more important than the physical handling of the product was the actual sale of films.[40]

While in most industries customers know the quality of the goods they are purchasing, the film industry operated on the principle of "blind-booking," at least until the practice was outlawed in 1948. Distribution sent sales representatives "into the field" every spring to sell the company's total production output for a given year. Sometime in May, Distribution sales personnel met at a national convention and were briefed on advertising strategies and sales pitches. By late summer, individual exhibitors and chains had usually signed contracts for groups of films which they planned to exhibit the following year. In most cases the commodity being sold had not yet been produced, in some cases the title, plot or director were known, in other cases only a star was named.

While exhibitors were not necessarily happy with this process, there was little they could do about it, since the practice was universal among the major companies. The interlocking nature of the film business created a rigid set of dependencies. An individual exhibitor could hardly afford to be blacklisted by distributors. On the other hand, if a

38. "Warner Salesmen Smash Through in Drive to Meet Company Crisis," in: *Sales Management*, Vol. 32, No. 3 (Feb. 1, 1933), p. 120; "Know-What-You're-Getting Plan Rejuvenates Warner 'Dealers'," in: *Sales Management*, Vol. 31, No. 7 (Oct. 1, 1932), p. 278.
39. Domestic exchanges were located in Albany, Atlanta, Boston, Buffalo, Charlotte, Chicago, Cincinnati, Cleveland, Dallas, Denver, Des Moines, Detroit, Indianapolis, Kansas City, Los Angeles, Memphis, Milwaukee, Minneapolis, New Haven, New Orleans, New York, Oklahoma City, Omaha, Philadelphia, Pittsburgh, Portland, Salt Lake City, San Francisco, Seattle, St. Louis, and Washington, D.C., *Warner Brothers Pictures: A Financial Review and Brief History 1923-1945*, Stockholders Report, 1945, Box 12706, Warner Brothers Archive, Princeton University (WB/PRI).
40. Ned E. Depinet: "The Problems of Motion Picture Distribution," in: *National Board of Review Magazine*, Vol. 3, No. 4 (April 1928), p. 4.

production company or distributor had wished to change such practices, he would have been stopped by the other majors, who would have either denied access to their first-run theatres, or refused to give the offending company films for its own theatres.

The actual pricing of individual films was also totally arbitrary, dependent on bargaining between a distribution salesperson and an exhibitor:

> *What the exhibitor has paid in the past for similar pictures, what the salesman thinks he should (or can be made) to pay, the type of picture under consideration, the number of the particular distributor's pictures the exhibitor is willing to take, the type of theatre in which the picture is to be shown, the amount of competition met with in that area, are only some of the factors influencing the final determination of terms.*[41]

One of the axioms of the film industry was: "Time is what we sell," which meant that the age of a film was in direct proportion to its selling price. Audiences were willing to pay higher prices for "first run" films than for older films. As a result, rentals for exactly the same film could vary between $10 and $10,000, depending on how many weeks the film had already been in general release. Approximately 50% of a film's total revenues were in fact earned in the first ninety days after release.[42]

Even when sales of an individual film were not sufficient to recoup studio investment, two other practices practically guaranteed film company profits: "block booking" and "grading." The latter meant that individual films were graded, according to the initial investment of the studio and their potential for box office success. The bigger the budget, the more stars the film offered, the higher its grading. The higher its grading, the greater the guarantee paid by the exhibitor and the bigger the cut given to the distributor. Thus, in the 1938-1939 season Warner Brothers designated seven films in group "A," demanding 35% of gross receipts from the exhibitor:[43]

1. *FOUR DAUGHTERS* with Claude Rains, the Lane Sisters
2. *DODGE CITY* with Errol Flynn, Olivia de Havilland
3. *ANGELS WITH DIRTY FACES* with James Cagney
4. *DAWN PATROL* with Errol Flynn
5. *DARK VICTORY* with Bette Davis
6. *JUAREZ* with Paul Muni
7. *EACH DAWN I DIE* with James Cagney, George Raft

Seven films in the "B" group at thirty percent of the gross included *CONFESSIONS OF A NAZI SPY* with Edward G. Robinson; fourteen films in the "C" group at 25%, including *GARDEN OF THE MOON* with Pat O'Brien; twenty-four films in the "D" group at twenty percent, including *NANCY DREW, REPORTER* with Bonita Granville. Because "C" and "D" films were less likely to generate substantial box office receipts, distributors

41. H.T. Lewis: "Distributing Motion Pictures," in: *Harvard Business Review*, Vol. 8, No. 3 (April 1929), p. 276.
42. Lewis, p. 201.
43. Warner Designations 1938-1939 Season, Distribution File, Box # 15499, WB/PRI.

Exhibitor's press book for THE MYSTERY OF THE WAX MUSEUM (1933).

could afford to accept lower percentage points. As most exhibitors were less enthusiastic about renting Nancy Drew and Torchy Blane films, given the low returns, distributors made block booking compulsory.

Block booking meant that an exhibitor could not rent films on an individual basis from a distributor, but was forced instead to purchase a complete package, sight unseen, at an aggregate price. Such a block included its share of "B," "C," and "D" films. Thus, a cinema in New York in 1937, for example, would be forced to buy not just one film with Paul Muni, but thirty films with Paul Muni, Barbara Stanwyck, George Arliss, Ann Dvorak, Douglas Fairbanks Jr., William Powell, Kay Francis, James Cagney, and "to be announced," paying a $100-125 up-front guarantee per film. Warner Brothers received $3,300 cash, before even one film had seen the light of a projector lamp. In many cases, the exhibitor was also required to buy all short subjects, cartoons, newsreels, and trailers, if he hoped to rent a desirable feature.[44]

44. Warner Brothers Productions Schedule of Exhibitions Contract, Park Lane Theatre, NYC, September 1937, Box # 14280, WB/PRI.

Needless to say, the company could practically finance a year's production with accumulated guarantees, while placing the burden of financial risk firmly in the lap of the exhibitor. Distributors peddled inferior films, made at virtually no cost above studio overhead, while demanding an inflated price for those films as a *quid pro quo* for supplying "A" films. The cost to the distributor of advertising was also substantially lowered, since marketing efforts were not needed for every single film, but only for the blockbusters: it was estimated that selling films on an individual basis would have increased costs by as much as fifty to seventy-five percent.[45]

Refusal to rent an entire block usually resulted in an exhibitor being blacklisted and having henceforth to acquire films from an independent, "States Rights" distributor. The latter usually only had rights to "C" and "D" films, made by poverty-row studios. Block booking effectively closed the market to independent producers, since the blocks of the major companies absorbed virtually all the limited playing time of an exhibitor. Between 1921 and 1948 the Federal Trade Commission, the U.S. Justice Department, and the various House and Senate sub-committees on interstate commerce tried almost continuously to have the practice of block booking outlawed, without success.

Distribution companies also practiced what was called "designated play dates." According to this scheme, the distributor could demand of exhibitors that certain films be played on certain days of the week. Naturally, a distributor would want to have "A" films play on weekends, when attendance and receipts could be expected to be highest. Major distributors demanded that their films receive preferential treatment, thus forcing exhibitors to program the films of independent producers on the days of lowest attendance. Only the larger movie theatre chains were powerful enough to reject such interference in the management of their businesses.

Finally, the distributors of the majors practiced a system of "zoning," euphemistically called "protection," whereby individual movie theatres were graded, according to location and audience. The purpose of the practice was clearly to protect one set of theatres from the competition of another. First run theatres were allowed to keep a film for a certain period of time, a "run." Then, a specified period of time, a "clearance," had to be observed, before a film could be given to another "second run" movie house. As a result of this system, an individual theatre could only rent a film after it had played in other theatres zoned above it, and before those theatres zoned below it, regardless of how much money an exhibitor was willing to pay.

Every year Distribution set up an extremely specific "Clearance Schedule." For example, in the Washington D.C. area in 1944-45, the Savoy Theatre, a second run house under the first run Earle and Ambassador Theatres, was zoned to receive a film twenty-one days after its initial run. The Tivoli picked up a film two weeks after the Savoy, followed in two more weeks by the Sheridan. Below the Sheridan were the Kennedy, the Colony, and the York. Theatres in the towns of Rockville, Silver Springs, Falls Church,

---

45. Huettig, p. 122. See also P.S. Harrison: "Give the Movie Exhibitor a Chance!" in: *Christian Century*, Vol. 52, No. 25 (June 25, 1935), pp. 819-821.

Gaithersburg, Capitol Heights, and Bethesda were also expected to wait at least three weeks after the first run ended, before they could book a film.[46] A seventh run, therefore, was likely not to be scheduled until 133 days after the end of the first run. After approximately six months, the film would be available for a fifteen-cent admission.[47]

As a result of this policy, theatres in some neighborhoods, for example, those whose audience was predominantly working class or black, would not get films until six months to a year after their original release. Theatres in some towns were given preference over theatres in other towns. This was the case, even if the theatre in question was newer, more attractive, and more comfortable than competing theatres with better zone ratings: "Classification of theatres with respect to run, clearance, and zoning was generally uniform and definitive as far as all the majors were concerned."[48]

An exhibitor's earning power for a film was directly related to its number of weeks in release, since a manager could hardly charge first run ticket prices for second run films. While the zone ultimately determined the percentage a distributor demanded, the distributor usually required only a flat fee for third, fourth, and fifth runs, since earnings could be expected to be extremely low. As a result, the five majors who controlled only a fraction of all the theatres in the United States, but 77% of all first run theatres, earned a total of 90% of all film rentals.[49] Furthermore, Warner Brothers directly controlled only 560 theatres, which meant it had to convince both theatres affiliated with the other majors and independents to buy their product. This is where publicity and advertising played its biggest role.

46. Clearance Schedule for Penn Theatre, Washington, D.C., October 26, 1944, Box # 14329, USC/PRI.
47. Charles P. Skouras: "The Exhibitor," in: *The Annals of the American Academy of Political and Social Science*, Vol. 254 (November 1947), p. 29.
48. Huettig, p. 127.
49. Dawson (1948), p. 230.

The development of a consumer culture in the United States had its origins in the institutionalization of the mass production of goods and services and the concomitant need to find markets for those goods. If a Henry Ford, for example, was going to make automobiles on an assembly line, producing thousands of cars a year, he had to convince American consumers that they needed to have a "Model T," if they hoped to live well. Through modern advertising techniques, through the sophisticated use of words and images, consumerism found its voice in American life, creating the illusion that social equality was a matter of saving enough money to purchase goods. "The elevation of the goods and values of mass production to the realm of a truth was a primary task among those who sought to educate the masses to the logic of consumerism."[50] The film industry served as both a handmaiden to consumer culture and was itself a constituent part of it. It directly marketed its own products, and indirectly those of American industry.

As early as 1911, *The Moving Picture World*, an industry trade periodical, advised its film industry readers to avail themselves of modern advertising techniques, in order to improve box office receipts, noting that:

> *... if the enterprising theatre manager will study the four cardinal*
> *points of theatre management, i.e. Welfare, Comfort, Entertainment,*
> *and Advertising, developing and perfecting them all in a systematic*
> *way, he will quickly solve the problem of box office success.*[51]

The article further suggested that advertising could take various forms, including slides, posters, photographs in lobby cases, and souvenirs. Even more surprising, the piece called for "long distance" advertising, such as wall posters, circulars, postcards, form letters, and newspaper advertisements. Thus, advertising came to cinema, especially in the form of posters and film stills, almost simultaneously with the birth of the medium.[52]

By the mid-1920s, publicity was a "high art." The publicity machine went into operation the moment a film began production and continued until the public premieres and first runs had taken place. Producers and distributors realized that a film's financial success depended on word-of-mouth and coverage generated in the press. Publicity could increase box office receipts by anywhere from five to fifteen percent.[53] As a result,

50. Ewen, p. 69.
51. George Rockhill Craw: "Swelling the Box Office Receipts - Advertising the Theatre," in: *Moving Picture World*, Vol. 8, No. 20 (May 20, 1911), pp. 1117-1118.
52. See also "The Poster End," in: *Moving Picture World*, Vol. 5, No. 22 (Nov. 27, 1909), p. 752; "Photographs of Moving Picture Actors - A New Method of Lobby Advertising," in: *Moving Picture World*, Vol. 6, No. 2 (Jan. 15, 1910), p. 50.
53. Lynn Farnol: "Hollywood Build-up," in: *Theatre Arts*, Vol. 25, No. 4 (April 1941), p. 297.

distributors were increasingly more willing to share the burden of advertising with exhibitors, spending no less than $50,000 to $75,000 per film in 1925.[54] By the early 1940s the industry was spending an estimated $100 million on advertising a year. A clause was written into the standard exhibition contract, making it mandatory for theatre owners to purchase and utilize publicity materials produced by the distributor. Naturally, these were sold to theatre managers at a profit.

The publicity build-up began as soon as a film went into production. Each film was assigned a unit publicist whose sole job it was to place stories about the production and its stars in the press, especially the fan magazines. Whether these stories were true or not mattered little. In the publicity hierarchy, the unit publicist was on its lowest rung, followed by the exploitation man, whose job it was to create publicity stunts. Nothing was too outrageous if it got some attention. Thus, for THE LIFE OF EMILE ZOLA (1937), Charles Einfeld, Head of W.B. Publicity, reported that "one hundred and one events have taken place in connection with the launching of this great attraction," including a MARCH OF TIME program, a cover on Time magazine, a medal from Parents magazine, speeches and lectures at Jewish organizations, radio programs on English and Hebrew language stations, as well as a premiere with "the greatest aggregate of society, literary, dramatic and civic leaders ever put under one roof."[55] Press agents never stopped believing their own hype, even when reporting to the boss.

Premieres offered major opportunities for significant press coverage. The more glamorous a world premiere, the more stars and other personalities could be brought into a theatre, the greater the subsequent outreach. But premieres were not always staged on Hollywood Boulevard or Broadway. For SANTE FE TRAIL (1940), W.B. publicity organized a whistle stop tour from Los Angeles to Sante Fe, New Mexico, loading the whole cast, the press corps and dozens of other screen personalities on a specially scheduled train. Before the world premieres at three local theatres, various members of the SANTE FE TRAIL cast attended: a "Luminarias" bonfire festival, a sand-painting exhibition, a piñon nut eating contest, a "gran Baile," a pow-wow with representatives from eight Southwestern Native American tribes, a parade, a ski party at Sante Fe National Forest, and the burning-in-effigy of the "God of Gloom."[56]

Personal appearance tours were in fact another marketing strategy of the studios, ever-conscious of publicity "stunts." While on tour, actors received their regular salaries, plus expenses. Hollywood stars in the flesh could increase a film's box office receipts by as much as forty percent. Thus it was hardly surprising that the film companies demanded the presence of its stars not only at premieres, but also at road shows, often asking an actor to make five or six appearances a day.[57] Parades, look-alike contests,

54. Rufus Steele: "Exploiters Magnificent," in: The Outlook, Vol. 140, No. 11 (July 15, 1925), pp. 393-396.
55. Letter Charles Einfeld to Jack Warner, August 11, 1937, Box 2817, WB/USC.
56. SANTA FE TRAIL, publicity releases, Box #683, WB/USC. See also Michael Costello: "They Pronounce It Pre-meer," in: The Commonweal, Vol. 33, No. 12 (January 10, 1941), p. 294.
57. "In the Flesh," in Time, Vol. 54, No. 27 (November 21, 1949).

festivals, birthday parties, historical recreations, sports events, anything was fair game to get a star into the Hinterlands, and the name of his or her newest film into the press.

Ironically, while these events were highly-orchestrated, artificial media events, whose purpose was clearly to generate publicity and ultimately to sell tickets at the box office, they did afford a very real opportunity for audience participation. Not only did they permit fans and autograph hounds a close look at the objects of their most intense desires, they also bestowed upon ordinary citizens a moment of glory, as they appeared on stage or in parades with their idols. This sense of belonging to a community of like-minded individuals was an important strategy in advertising, and could be used to fuel the desire for more movies.

Warner Brothers' Publicity published its own news and features service, *Hollywood News*, in order to keep a steady stream of information flowing to the press. Once a film was ready for release, theatre owners were sent press books, which not only included ready-made articles for placement in local newspapers, but also descriptions of "campaigns" which could be organized on a local level, often involving the Boy Scouts or other civic groups. "Articles" detailed the history of a production, mishaps that may have occurred, the extreme financial and human effort put out by cast and crew, individual biographies of the principals, and historical background on the subject of the film, etc. The pressbook also included photos and galleys of advertisements, which could be placed in local papers, as well as poster designs, lobby card motifs, and suggestions for lobby displays.

Given the hyperbole of movie publicity, it was not surprising that the film industry itself made an effort, at least seemingly, to regulate cinema advertising. Film distributors inserted a clause in the standard exhibitor's contract, giving the former authority over all advertising decisions. In 1935 the industry's internal censorship bureau, the "Hays Office," instituted its own "Advertising Codes." Thereafter, Warner Brothers and other film companies voluntarily submitted all pressbooks, trade journal advertisements, posters, stills, and trailers to the Hays Office for approval.[58] While keeping the guardians of public morality mollified, this development served to legitimize advertising, giving it the appearance of being factual or truthful, just as the "truth in advertising" campaign of the 1910s only legitimized the advertising industry's own conception of honesty.[59]

The goal of advertising was not merely to sell movies, but also to propagate a consumerist "lifestyle" as a by-product of that sale. Very early on, filmmakers realized that movies could be used to advertise consumer goods, either directly or indirectly. They knew they could kill two birds with one stone, i.e., they could lower their own production costs by asking manufacturers to supply certain goods, which would appear in their movies, and they could earn additional income by licensing their stars for advertising.

58. John Elliot Williams: "They Stopped at Nothing," in: *Hollywood Quarterly*, Vol. 1, No. 3 (April 1946), pp. 273-4.
59. Ewen, p. 71.

The chorus of GOLD DIGGERS of 1937 is greeted at Dallas Airport by the local mayor.

Certainly hairstyles, clothing, make-up, and other personal grooming habits of ordinary Americans were influenced by the fashions the stars wore. It was not long before manufacturers paid for the privilege of having their products appear in films. Product tie-ins, as the film industry euphemistically called such advertising, was in general practice by the 1920s. Manufacturers hired agencies to represent them to the film companies, offering them as many props as necessary to get a plug in a new film.[60] The Ford Motor Company regularly sent their new models to the studios, with the result that Fords were the single most-often-seen cars in American film of the 1930s. Short subjects were often nothing more than extended advertisements for products, disguised as documentaries, travelogues, or cartoons. Manufacturers often financed such short films as *MY MERRIE OLDSMOBILE*, or more subtly, *ON THE SLOPES OF THE ANDES* (A&P Coffee).[61]

Furthermore, product tie-ins could be employed to sell both films and consumer products. For example, when a given film was based on a novel, publishers and film distributors were encouraged to have stills from the film on the book's cover, and references to the book in film advertising. Bookstores put together displays when the films adapted from literature opened. Likewise, shopkeepers were asked to create window displays linking their goods, whether they be pipes, sheet music, or drugs, to a film at the local cinema.

60. "Firms Get Free Ads in Movies," in *Business Week*, No. 522 (September 2, 1939). See also Oswell Blakeston: "The Tie-Up Comes of Age," in: *Sight and Sound*, Vol. 17, No. 67 (Autumn 1948), pp. 122-123.
61. "Cinemadvertising," in: *Time*, Vol. 17, No. 21 (May 25, 1931), p. 58.

29

On a national level, stars gave their likenesses to soap and Coke advertisers, who placed ads in newspapers, magazines and on billboards with a polite reference to the star's latest film. Such licensing of actors, or cartoon characters, usually generated considerable income for the film companies. The sale of Joe E. Brown's visage to Quaker Oats helped Warners out of its worst Depression year. Warner licensed its animated Looney Tunes and Merrie Melodies characters to the Acme Embroideries Company, and the voices of Bugs Bunny and Co. to Capitol Records. From Acme, Warners received a guarantee of $2,000 or five percent of all sales for a two year period, from Capitol a guarantee of $3,300 per album produced or 3.33% of sales.[62] Warner Brothers earned income both on the films they produced, and on the products which advertised their films. Thus, the dream merchants not only created demands for consumer goods, which promised to fulfill an audience's desire to belong to mainstream America, they also colluded with manufacturers to satisfy the demand created.

62. *Fortune* (1936), p. 210; Licensing Agreements, Warner Brothers Legal Department, Box #12675, WB/PRI.

I t was an industry truism that more money could be made in exhibition than in any other branch of the film industry. In 1946 in the United States, approximately 18,000 motion pictures theatres sold four billion admissions, adding up to an income of $1.66 billion, excluding Federal Admission Tax.[63] While the production and distribution ends of the industry employed approximately 32,000 persons, employment in America's movie houses reached 172,000.[64] The major film companies realized that corporate control of large theatre chains was a necessary ingredient for success. Paramount with over 1,500 cinemas was the undisputed giant, followed by Warners (557), 20th Century-Fox (538), RKO (132), and Loew's (122).[65]

Financial power was measured, however, not only by the number of theatres, but also by ownership of first run houses. The majors were undisputed in this regard. Competition between the majors, on the other hand, was practically nonexistent. They had divided up the country between themselves: Paramount controlled the South, North-Central, and New England regions; 20th Century-Fox's West Coast theatres dominated the Pacific and Mountain states; Warner Brothers strength lay in the Mid-Atlantic area; RKO controlled New York and New Jersey; Loew's Inc. ruled around New York City. Thus, it was in exhibition that the government's anti-trust case could be most convincingly proven:

> *The division of the exhibition branch of the industry into separate areas of control has not only eliminated competition in exhibition between the major companies, but also made each major company the dominant element in every territory in which it operates, even where opposed by powerful independent interests.*[66]

The organization and operation of giant movie theatre chains in the 1920s was modeled on the chain store strategy, as developed by American retailers.[67] Food store chains, like A&P, variety stores, like Woolworth and Kresge, and other retailers for clothing, gas stations, and drug stores applied the same principles of scientific management to selling consumer goods that industry used in manufacturing. By centralizing

---

63. Floyd B. Odlum: "Financial Organization of the Motion Picture Industry," in: *The Annals of the American Academy of Political and Social Sciences. The Motion Picture Industry*, Vol. 254 (November 1947), p. 18.
4. Glover and Cornell, p. 950.
65. Figures for 1948, quoted in Dawson (1948), p. 228.
66. TNEC Monograph No. 43, *The Motion Picture - a Pattern of Control*, 1941, quoted in: Robert A. Brady: "The Problem of Monopoly," in: *The Annals of the American Academy of Political and Social Sciences*, Vol. 254 (November 1947), p. 129.
67. Douglas Gomery: "The Movies Become Big Business: Public Theatres and the Chain Store Strategy," in: *Cinema Journal*, Vol. 18, No. 2 (Spring 1979), p. 26. This whole section is indebted to Gomery's pioneering research.

management, and distribution, by purchasing goods in quantity, by spreading fixed costs, chain store operations could lower overhead and maximize profits. Utilizing similar strategies, theatre chains decreased operating costs. Management of Warners' chain was situated in New York, where other decisions concerning everything from advertising to concessions were made. Furthermore, theatre chains had more leverage with distributors, because they required product for hundreds of screens, allowing them to make more advantageous rental deals with distributors. Finally, the distribution companies of the majors gave preferential treatment to Warners' theatre chains as a *quid pro quo* for equal treatment of their theatres by Warners' Distribution.

The first run movie palaces were not only operated according to modern principles of management, but also employed highly specialized personnel. Staff in the largest houses was divided into no less than twelve departments:[68]

1. Manager's office	7. Stage department
2. Service department	8. Musical department
3. Housekeeping department	9. Advertising department
4. Engineering department	10. Accounting department
5. Production department	11. Sign department
6. Projection department	12. Tailoring department

Some departments dealt with the front of the theatre, i.e. with the public, while others worked in back, i.e. in projection, housekeeping, and maintenance. The service staff included floor managers, ushers, elevator operators, page boys, doormen, streetmen, footmen, box office "girls," nurses, and matrons. Housekeeping included superintendents, porters, janitors, and maids. Each staff person wore a different uniform, making them easily identifiable to the public. Uniforms were often designed to match the decor of the theatre and were expected to be spotless and freshly pressed. Particularly large houses employed as many as fifty boys as ushers.[69]

In the classical era of Hollywood cinema, first run movie palaces exuded class, hoping to lure patrons into their 2,000 to 3,000 seat temples of entertainment. In the 1920s exhibitors discovered the advantages in offering air conditioning to a populace attempting to beat the summer heat.[70] For the privilege of seeing films in luxurious surroundings, audiences were required to pay substantially higher ticket prices. In the lobbies of many theatres the customer was first greeted by a battery of ushers. The lobbies themselves were usually spacious, featuring displays, posters, stills, and lobby cards advertising up-coming events. Sometimes, at the suggestion of the press book supplied by the distributor, the theatre manager would organize a special exhibit which tied-in to the main attraction. When the Depression put a financial squeeze on exhibitors,

---

68. Harold B. Franklin, *Motion Picture Theater Management* (New York: George H. Doran Company, 1927) p. 49.
69. Franklin, pp. 179-180.
70. Gomery, (1979), p. 29.

The Wales was a typical Warners Theatre in a provincial town, offering films months after their initial release.

staffs were cut, and concessions, especially popcorn and candy, were introduced to augment ticket sales. With profit margins of better than 100%, concessions stands proved to be a boom to the exhibition end of the industry.[71] In some theatres, managers set up juke boxes in the corners, allowing teens to "hang out" when they got bored with the fare on screen. Other shorter-lived methods of overcoming slow sales included so-called "Bank Nights," which were thinly-veiled lotteries with cash prizes, and "Premium Nights," on which patrons received inexpensive china, linens, flatware, and other household goods.[72]

The average movie theatre rented approximately 175 features and 350 short subjects per year.[73] A typical program began with a newsreel, followed by a cartoon or other short subject, and the feature presentation, rounding out the average two-hour cycle. In the largest first run houses, film programs were often introduced with musical overtures and stage shows, although live entertainment fell off with the advent of the Depression. In the 1920s, theatres began presenting double features and, in some cases triple features, expanding an evening at the pictures to almost three hours.

By the early 1940s, nearly three-quarters of all movie theatres showed double-

71. Gomery, (1986), p. 21.
72. "Premium Thriller," in: *Business Week*, No. 275 (December 8, 1934, p. 24; "Bank Night," in: *Time*, Vol. 27, No. 5 (February 3, 1936); "Bank Night," in: *The New Republic*, Vol. 86, No. 1118 (May 6, 1936), p. 363; Pare Lorentz: "Movie Platform," in: *The Digest*, Vol. 1, No. 4 (August 7, 1937), p. 23.
73. Franklin,(1927), p. 28.
74. Edward R. Beach: "Double Features in Motion Picture Exhibition," in: *Harvard Business Review*, Vol. 10, No. 4 (July 1932), pp. 505-515; Frank S. Nugent: "Double, Double, Toil and Trouble," in: *New York Times Magazine*, January 17, 1943, p. 11.

bills.[74] Following the requisite newsreel and shorts, the first feature on a double bill was usually a "B" or "C" film. Only then were patrons treated to the top-billed "A" film. The controversy over double-billing raged for twenty years, with the industry itself usually maintaining that the practice increased revenues. Indeed, theatres offering doubles usually fared better than did their single feature rivals. Nevertheless, public opinion polls demonstrated that the American public as a whole actually showed a slight preference for single feature programs. Teens and working class patrons, on the other hand, favored doubles.[75]

Long before opinion polling became a standard practice in American life, the film companies were test marketing their films. Previews of feature films, usually scheduled in selected theatres which demonstrated desirable demographics, were a matter of course by the early 1930s. At previews, patrons filled out prepared audience-reaction cards, or managers were assigned to eavesdrop on patrons leaving the theatre. A typical audience reaction report would quote a variety of comments, e.g. "The best acting I've seen in a long time," or "The sound was perfect to the ears."[76] If a film previewed poorly, the studio often decided to recut it, or (in some cases) reshot material, after some emergency script-doctoring.

Despite the monopolization of the film marketplace, which did substantially limit audience choices to those products offered by the major studios, audiences were not totally powerless. Movie patrons did reject films, causing them to fail financially, despite all the manipulation through advertising, despite the endless publicity hype, despite consumer-oriented product advertising. In spite of the film companies' seemingly rigid programming of audience reactions, movie-goers did manage to make the cinema a participatory event. Against the over-determined narratives of Hollywood, film fans created their own in scrapbooks, pasting cut-up fan magazines with imaginative flair. Using film studio-produced "study guides" in conjunction with screenings of literary adaptations, English teachers sometimes made great novels and plays accessible to students who might otherwise not have bothered. By participating in look-alike contests or the parades of the stars, patrons dared to imagine their own aspirations, finding reinforcement in neighbors at their side.

While the film companies orchestrated public events in the interests of advertising, mass audiences came together, interacted socially, found friends, established a sense of community. Their usage of film events against the grain of the studios' publicity hounds, e.g., to search out their historical roots on *DODGE CITY*'s prairie, was a mark of their freedom. Like the film viewing experience itself, which could not prevent a great deal of collective subjectivity, audiences reacted in unison, as if all in the same dream. That the mass audience medium of cinema has given way to the mass isolation of television, is a measure of the dreams we've lost.

75. Quoted in Leo A. Handel: *Hollywood looks at its audience* (Urbana: University of Illinois Press, 1950), p. 131.
76. A MIDSUMMER NIGHT'S DREAM (1935), legal file, Box #2876, WB/USC.

34

The Hollywood studio system was self-sufficient, carefully organized to maximize efficiency. Thousands of people worked there every day.

The studios were cities within cities, both real sites of labor and potemkin villages, like this Western street scene.

*Studio lunch counter
where blue collar
workers ate.*

*Child actors learning
with studio teacher
between takes of
ANTHONY ADVERSE
(1936).*

*The studio
Transportation
Department functioned
as a local garage.*

*The studio Fire
Department answered
alarms both on the
backlot and off, and was
responsible for
maintaining safety
standards during
production.*

The studio Infirmary treated both emergency patients and gave studio personnel periodic physicals.

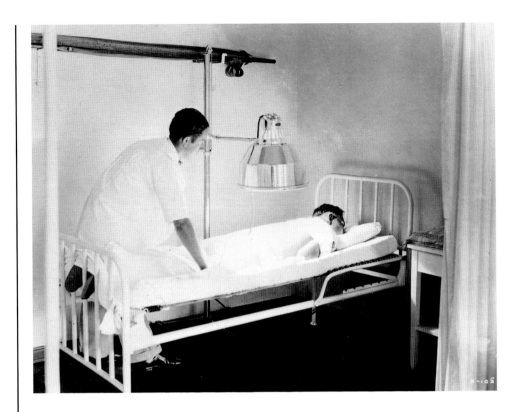

The Warner Brothers: Lewis, Jack, Harry and Albert with Bobby Jones (middle). Jack controlled the studio, but Harry held the real power in the New York office, while Albert ostensibly was responsible for distribution.

Studio producers, like B-film specialist Bryan Foy, supervised Warners' films all along the assembly line, from script development through post-production.

As many as ten scriptwriters were involved in writing a film. Each succeeding draft was approved and reproduced for further work.

Completed scripts, scheduled for production, were sent to the Research Department, where historical details, costumes, and other facts (such as names and dates) were checked for accuracy.

Costume designs were not only for films, but also for fashions, which were then sold to the public through retailers.

Costume designs were passed on to tailors, cutters, and seamstresses who worked full-time in the studio's own sweat shop.

Errol Flynn gets a fitting for CAPTAIN BLOOD (1935).

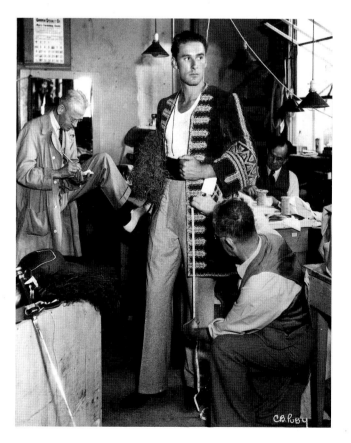

After designing sets, art directors built 3-D models before actual set construction began. Here Max Reinhardt, William Dieterle and Anton Grot discuss set for A MIDSUMMER NIGHT'S DREAM (1935).

Carpenters, metalworkers and painters worked on the construction of both interior and exterior sets.

Even when sets were reused, painters were hired to give them a fresh coat, or (as in this case) to make them look "worn."

The plaster shop reconstructed statues, monuments or any other set elements needed to give the scene a realistic look.

Studio scripts, as well as all studio publicity, posters, and press materials, were produced in the print shop.

The Prop Department stored and made available all props used during film production, including this array of firearms.

This short leading man gets a lift from the Prop Department.

Make-up artists designed facial features for all actors, an especially important job when actors had to look older or younger than their actual ages.

*While some actors
applied their own make-
up before a shoot, others
relied on specialists to
achieve the desired
effects.*

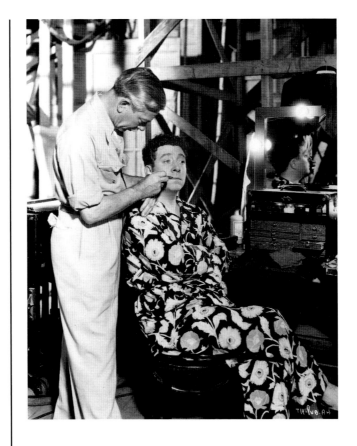

*The Make-Up
Department was also
responsible for special
effects, such as James
Cagney's donkey-head
for A MIDSUMMER
NIGHTS DREAM.
(1935).*

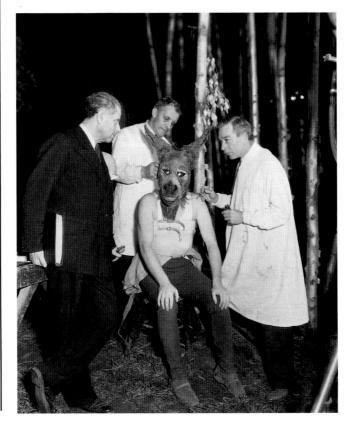

46

Once the sets were built, the lighting crew went to work to create the proper atmosphere, using sometimes hundreds of lamps for complicated production shots.

Cinematographer Sol Polito and his assistants with a special camera mounted on a suspensor for stability and mobility.

The focus puller and grip assisted the cameraman by measuring the exact distance between the camera and actors.

In the sound control room technicians could monitor sound on a number of different sound stages at the same time.

After the introduction of sound in 1927, the soundman became almost as important as the cameraman, since he was responsible for recording audible dialogue.

At the first production meeting, the producer, director, actors and crew met to go over the script.

49

Rehearsals were important to some directors, not to others. Here Sam Wood rehearses a scene with Ingrid Bergman and Gary Cooper for SARATOGA TRUNK (1946).

Before shooting musicals or other films with song and dance, chorus and dancers underwent intensive training with a dance director.

Extra talent was hired from among Hollywood's 15,000 to 20,000 extras, many of whom worked only marginally, and for extremely low wages.

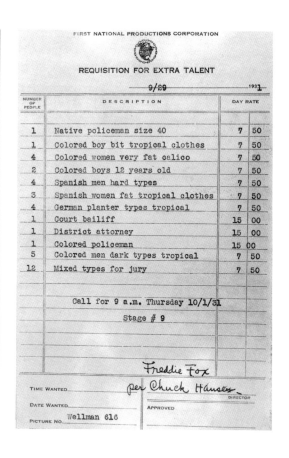

FIRST NATIONAL PRODUCTIONS CORPORATION

REQUISITION FOR EXTRA TALENT

9/29 _____ 1931

NUMBER OF PEOPLE	DESCRIPTION	DAY RATE	
1	Native policeman size 40	7	50
1	Colored boy bit tropical clothes	7	50
4	Colored women very fat calico	7	50
2	Colored boys 12 years old	7	50
4	Spanish men hard types	7	50
3	Spanish women fat tropical clothes	7	50
4	German planter types tropical	7	50
1	Court bailiff	15	00
1	District attorney	15	00
1	Colored policeman	15	00
5	Colored men dark types tropical	7	50
12	Mixed types for jury	7	50

Call for 9 a.m. Thursday 10/1/31

Stage # 9

Freddie Fox
per Chuck Hansen
DIRECTOR

TIME WANTED _____

DATE WANTED _____   APPROVED _____

PICTURE NO. Wellman 616

Between scenes actors spent a lot of time just sitting and waiting for the next shot to be set up. Here Ingrid Bergman passes the time by shooting her own home movies.

Actors were required to pose continuously for publicity shots, in order to satisfy the virtually insatiable demand of the fan magazines. Here Doris Day checks stills while waiting between takes for MY DREAM IS YOURS (1949).

Major actors and actresses always had stand-ins to appear in the long shots or reverse angles, or when they could not be on the set. Here May Robson with her look-alike, Mary Warren.

The work of stuntmen was often extremely dangerous and sometimes fatal. As free-lancers, they received neither unemployment compensation, nor pensions for disabilities.

Animal actors were a little more difficult to handle than their human counterparts, but ultimately cheaper. Here the "Noah's Ark" sequence is being prepared for GREEN PASTURES (1936).

Close-ups of car chases were usually shot in the studio with rear-projection, since this method was infinitely cheaper than taking a crew out on location into real city streets.

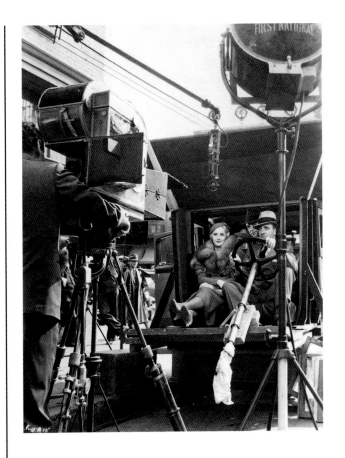

On Warners' huge sound stages, whole worlds could be created with plaster, lumber, canvas, and light. The tracks allowed for the camera to travel smoothly and steadily through this pastoral landscape for SERGEANT YORK (1941).

*Technicians created
"real" snow from
cornflakes and goose
feathers for this winter
scene from WHITE
BANNERS (1938).*

*For spectacular scenes
film crews often went out
on location, completing
dangerous shots, such as
this one for Rin Tin Tin's
THE IVORY TRAIL
(1930).*

*Working with a moviola,
editor Irene Morra cuts
the film according to
directions from the
producer. In Hollywood,
editing was traditionally
"woman's work."*

*Recording music for the
SEA HAWK (1940), the
orchestra followed the
musical director, who
kept one eye on the
screen behind the
musicians.*

The Animation Department at Warner Brothers was a business all its own. Cartoons involved highly labor-intensive cel animation, the coloring of which was mostly done by low-paid female workers.

Blacks working at Warner Brothers were (as in society generally) invisible, serving as messengers, maids or food service workers.

Blacks appearing in front of the camera were often seen in highly stereo-typed bit comedy parts, or as nothing more than a chorus of happy-go-lucky singers, as here in THE SINGING KID (1936).

Around the country Warner Brothers owned distribution outlets, called "exchanges," from which prints were then delivered to the theatres.

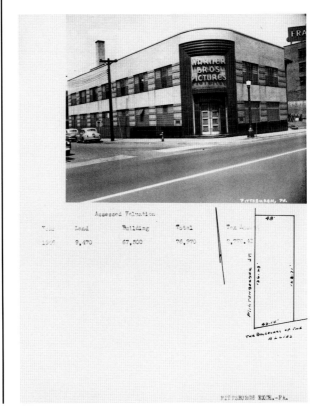

The Photography Department worked hand-in-hand with the studio Publicity Department to document the whole process of film production, as well as the subsequent publicity campaigns, especially if these involved "stars" mixing with ordinary fans.

Certain stars favored certain portrait photographers who could show them in their best light. Each photographer had his own style and method of working. Here Kay Francis gets the build-up.

KFWB was the local Warners-owned radio station in Los Angeles. Warner Brothers was a communications conglomerate, owning radio stations, as well as radio manufacturing companies, publishing interests, theatre supply houses and Broadway theatre productions.

In order to sell products to exhibitors, the Publicity Department organized bi-annual conventions of theatre owners, where the latter were given previews of the following year's films, as well as instruction in the best methods of advertising.

Before a new film opened, the Publicity Department would flood the country with all manner of print material, using every kind of media, including milk bottles.

Public events surrounding publicity campaigns were a favorite way to lure patrons into the theatre. These included look-alike contests, bank nights, door prizes, bingo contests, cutlery and cookware give-aways, and parades.

61

Personal appearance tours could be tied-in to contests and premieres of new films.

Radio tie-ins were used to publicize films and the accompanying contests and premieres.

Billboards were an often-used medium for advertising.

Billboards were relatively inexpensive and could reach large numbers of viewers in an age before television.

Personal appearance tours were scheduled by studio publicity before every film premiere, since they offered "events" for the press, which would help publicize the film.

Mobbed by fans looking for autographs or souvenirs, the life of an actor on tour was often gruelling. Actors had little choice, though, since their contracts usually stipulated that they make themselves available for publicity.

Keeping their names in the public eye and in the press was the most important aspect of an actor's work, if he or she hoped to continue being successful.

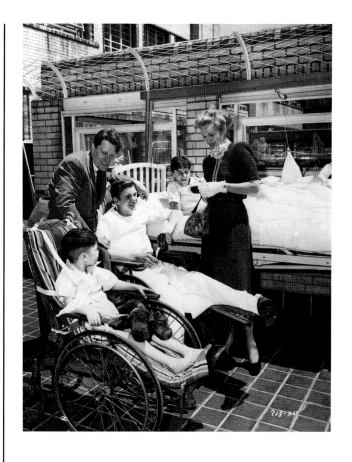

Everybody loves a parade. The excitement of parades offered spectators a taste of what was to come in the theatre.

The big premieres brought out the stars and the press, which meant free publicity in the morning papers.

Crowds of onlookers often became extremely agitated when a well-known star came into view.

Warner Brothers owned over 500 movie houses, including the flagship Warner Brothers Theatre in Beverly Hills.

The Carthay was another first run theatre owned by Warners in Los Angeles.

The Beverly Theatre was a second run house, owned by Warner Brothers in Washington, DC.

```
1946 Assessed Valuation        6,975
Tax Amount          122.08
```

During World War II soldiers seldom went without their weekly movie fix, frequenting temporary theatres within miles of the front, and seeing films first run, supplied free of charge by the film companies.

The Warners' Theatre on Broadway featured huge marquees with artistic designs to attract attention.

Box offices and entrances to movie palaces were all flashing lights and colorful displays, enticing passers-by to partake in dreams.

Once inside the "palace," audiences were greeted by hoards of ushers, air conditioning and a promise of "the good life."

It was not until the Depression that theatre owners discovered concessions as a way to make more money. Concessions were, in fact, more profitable than ticket sales, since the earnings did not have to be split with distributors.

Large lobby displays
advertised forthcoming
films or served other
propagandistic and
educational ends, such
as this display for
*CONFESSIONS OF A
NAZI SPY* (1939).

Lobby cards advertised
coming attractions with
colorful scenes from the
film, even when the film
in question was in black
and white.

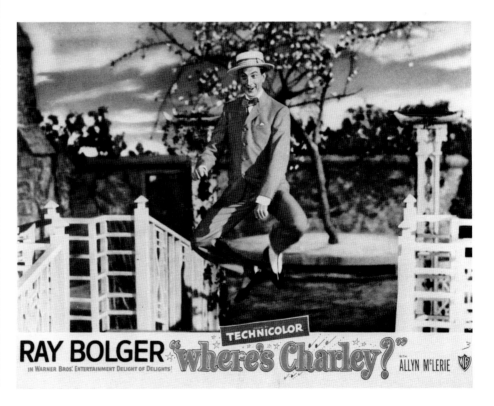

Another source of income for the company were product tie-ins, which sold both films and other consumer goods at the same time.

This Broadway Studebaker dealer tied-in his car to Warner's BABBITT in 1924.

Stars also earned extra income for the studio by giving their names and faces to consumer product advertising.

The licensing of products originating from films and cartoons proved to be a lucrative business.

In the classical golden age of Hollywood, the average American went to the movies at least once a week.

In 1945 the average American spent 45 cents of every entertainment dollar on the movies, dreaming in the dark.